BEING MAD, BEING GLAD

by Roger Day

Illustrated by Deborah Allwright

www.raintreepublishers.co.uk
Visit our website to find out more information about **Raintree** books.

To order:
 Phone 44 (0) 1865 888112
 Send a fax to 44 (0) 1865 314091
 Visit the Raintree bookshop at **www.raintreepublishers.co.uk** to browse our catalogue and order online.

First published in Great Britain by Raintree, Halley Court, Jordan Hill, Oxford OX2 8EJ, part of Harcourt Education.
Raintree is a registered trademark of Harcourt Education Ltd.

Raintree Editor: Kate Buckingham
Series Consultant: Dr Michele Elliott, Kidscape
Written by Roger Day
Illustrated by Deborah Allwright
Packaged by ticktock Media Ltd.
Designed by Robert Walster, BigBlu Design
Edited and project managed by Penny Worms

Printed and bound in China, by South China Printing

ISBN 1 844 43418 4
08 07 06 05 04
10 9 8 7 6 5 4 3 2 1

British Library Cataloguing in Publication Data
Day, Roger
Being mad, being glad. – (Kids' Guides)
155.4'124
A full catalogue record for this book is available from the British Library.

Every effort has been made to contact copyright holders of any material reproduced in this book. Any omissions will be rectified in subsequent printings if notice is given to the publishers.

All Internet addresses (URLs) given in this book were valid at the time of going to press. However, due to the dynamic nature of the Internet, some addresses may have changed, or sites may have changed or ceased to exist since publication. While the author and publishers regret any inconvenience this may cause readers, no responsibility for any such changes can be accepted by either the author or the publishers.

To my young advisers
Bethan, Siân, Sammy, Gideon, Nathanial and Miriam (RD)

CONTENTS

Introduction 4

Let's talk about...

Anger and fear 6

Jealousy and joy 8

Sadness and loneliness 10

True stories

I hate my brother 12

I miss my grandma 16

A new school 20

My clever best friend 24

What would you do? 28

Glossary 30

Find out more 31

Index 32

INTRODUCTION

This is a book about feelings. Our feelings are important. There are two kinds: **real feelings** and **cover-up feelings**.

The four real feelings are anger, fear, joy and sadness. We get sad about **painful loss**. We get angry to protect ourselves from harm or sort out problems. We feel fear now about things that might happen in the future. We feel joyful when we are relaxed and comfortable about the past, now and the future.

When I get angry, I want to run away or burst into tears.

I'm so happy I want to burst!

We have cover-up feelings, such as **jealousy** and **loneliness**, so we do not have to show or deal with how we really feel. Cover-up feelings leave us feeling bad or **confused**. A mum sounds angry when her child runs into the road. But she is probably feeling scared. A friend may speak horribly to you, but they might really be feeling sad about something that happened at home.

All my friends have got better toys. I wish I had new ones like them.

When I'm scared, my heart thumps fast.

It is best to show your real feelings so people can understand you and help you. If you can't, then talk to somebody. This book will show you how.

Let's talk about...
ANGER AND FEAR

> I want to hit something.

Anger is a release of **energy** that can help you sort out your problems or protect you from harm. You get angry when someone is hurting you or if something doesn't seem right or fair. When you are angry you can also get sulky or stroppy. You may want to damage things or hit people.

WHY DO I FEEL LIKE THIS?
Anger and fear are normal **emotions** and it is good to talk about them. It is not good to hurt people or things that matter.

Your anger affects other people, so find a safe way to let it out:

- write it down or draw it
- count to ten
- shout loudly
- kick a ball or run fast
- punch a pillow
- tear up unwanted paper.

BUT WHY ME?

You aren't the only one. Many people do not show their feelings. But they probably feel the same as you inside.

I'm scared!

People get afraid about the future, of **new situations** or of bad things happening to their family. Fear can give you trembly legs, tickles in your tummy or your heart might race.

I'm afraid of the dark.

Fear is a good thing, it stops you running into the road or walking off with a stranger. But some fears aren't helpful. You may be afraid of things that can't hurt you, such as thunder or scary movies.

LOOK AT IT ANOTHER WAY

Anger and fear are normal emotions. But sometimes when you have them, people find you difficult to deal with. If you have these feelings a lot, grown-ups may worry about you. Try to find good ways to let out your feelings.

If you feel scared, you can:
- watch something funny on TV
- ask a grown-up to say everything is okay
- turn scary change into exciting adventure.

Let's talk about...
JEALOUSY AND JOY

He gets everything he wants.

Jealousy is wanting to be like someone else. **Envy** is wanting things others have. These are **cover-up feelings** for anger. You may be jealous when someone else gets all the attention or be envious of a friend's toys. Jealous or envious people become unfriendly or want to spoil things.

I'm so jealous of my sister. Why didn't I have a party?

Here are some ways out of jealousy and envy:
- let out anger in a safe way
- remember life isn't always fair
- enjoy your own things
- think about good things people have said about you.

BUT WHY ME?

Most people get jealous sometimes. Find ways of turning jealousy into joy. Be grateful for your own things – some people have less than you. If you are happy, enjoy it!

Mum's got a great new boyfriend. He's taking us to Disneyland!

Joy is when people are happy with life and with what they have got. It is one of the nicest feelings you can have.

When you are joyful you may feel like dancing or shouting with excitement. Some people feel like bursting when they are happy. There are several things you can do:

- laugh, sing, dance and enjoy
- celebrate the way you are feeling right now
- when you have unhappy feelings, remember this time.

WHY DO I FEEL LIKE THIS?

If you are feeling jealous, often you think of nothing else. This is not a good feeling. Joy is being happy, excited and pleased, all at the same time.

LOOK AT IT ANOTHER WAY

When you are happy, other people may try to spoil your good feeling because they feel jealous. It may be better to save your excitement for when you are not with them.

Let's talk about...

SADNESS AND LONELINESS

People feel sad about losing something they can never get back. Someone may have died. You may have moved or your family's broken up. Sadness is a strong feeling. It is a good feeling even though it isn't nice. It is our way of saying goodbye. You may feel sad and then happy. You may have an empty feeling or pain inside.

It helps to:
- cry – you won't need to cry for ever
- talk to someone about how you feel
- draw or write about your feelings.

Sometimes I'm sad and get an empty feeling in my chest.

WHY DO I FEEL LIKE THIS?

Sadness is an empty feeling of loss. You cry until you are able to let go. Sometimes this takes a long time. Loneliness is usually sadness or fear in disguise.

BUT WHY ME?

Everyone feels sad when they lose someone or something. You feel lonely when you think no one cares about you.

Everyone wants to be alone sometimes. **Loneliness** is different. Lonely people feel on their own and sorry for themselves. They may want to hide away because they are sad. They may feel lonely when no one is near to them.

I'm lonely because I don't have any brothers and sisters to play with.

Let's swap! Sometimes I'd love to get away from my sisters and be on my own.

If you feel lonely:

- talk to someone about the way you feel
- tell people you want to be their friend
- discover ways to cheer yourself up
- find things to laugh and get excited about.

LOOK AT IT ANOTHER WAY

Some people try to hide their feelings. Grown-ups sometimes tell you: 'Big boys and girls don't cry.' If you push your feelings of sadness down inside you, one day they may burst out.

True stories

I HATE MY BROTHER

Hi! My name's Charlene. I'm from a Caribbean family. Mum and I used to get on really well and I loved it when she tucked me in at night and told me stories of **Jamaica**. But things have changed. My mum's always telling me off. It's all my brother Calvin's fault. He messes up my games, so I hit him. Then he goes crying to Mum and she shouts at me.

He messed up my picture!

I wish he'd never been born.

I hate my brother. He gets the attention and all the cuddles. I started shouting at Mum and hiding Calvin's things. Dad said I was being silly. I even dressed like a boy. After all, boys in my family are liked more. But I love my brother even though I hate him. What can I do?

What did you do to him?

I HATE MY BROTHER

Talking it through

It helps to talk to someone...

AN ADULT

Charlene's Aunt Josie says that it is okay to be angry and upset, but it's not okay to hurt Calvin. She suggests that when Charlene gets cross, she goes to her bedroom and punches her pillow.

A COUSIN

Her cousin Wilbert admits that Calvin can be annoying and gets a lot of the attention because of his age. He says that Charlene's family all love her and tells her to talk to her mum, then she will see.

A FRIEND

Her friend Megan says she likes playing with her little sister Lucy. She helps her to get dressed and reads her bedtime stories at night. Perhaps Charlene could do the same?

FORWARD STEPS

● TELL SOMEONE

Let a grown-up know when you are upset.

● EXPRESS YOUR FEELINGS

Get rid of your feelings without hurting others.

I decided to tell my mum how I felt. Mum put me on her lap and said I was still her precious little girl.

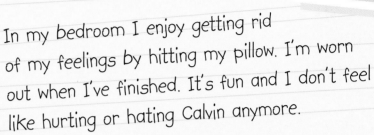

In my bedroom I enjoy getting rid of my feelings by hitting my pillow. I'm worn out when I've finished. It's fun and I don't feel like hurting or hating Calvin anymore.

Mum said she'd stop Calvin coming into my room when I'm playing, and she set up a star chart for when we play nicely together. I've got loads more stars than Calvin!

At night-time I go up to listen to Calvin's story. We both cuddle up to Mum. When Calvin is asleep, Mum braids my hair for school. She says it makes me look really pretty.

I MISS MY GRANDMA

Hi, I'm Jack and my little brother is called Harry. We get on all right, although sometimes we argue. We both agree on one thing: our grandma is the greatest. I like going to see her. We sit in her kitchen and she tells us funny stories about when she was little.

Harry and I cried when Mum said Grandma was dying. 'It isn't true,' I told her crossly.

Can't they do something to make her better?

Everyone dies at some point.

Now when I visit, Grandma is always in bed. She is thin and can't really talk. I asked her what would happen when she died. She said, 'My body will go and the real me will go up to heaven.'

Why does she have to die? Why can't she stay here for ever?

'What, like a rocket, Grandma?' I asked, remembering the rockets shooting up to the sky in our town's firework display.

'I expect so, Jack,' she whispered.

I MISS MY GRANDMA

Talking it through

It helps to talk to someone...

A PARENT

His dad says he knows how sad Jack is right now. Everyone is, but they have different ways of being sad. He tells Jack to find a special way to remember Grandma after she dies.

AN OLDER FRIEND

Jack's friend Joe knows how Jack is feeling. His cousin died in hospital after an accident. When she was dying, Joe used to sit in the big tree in the park and cry. Crying helped him.

A CLASSMATE

His friend Sophie says she doesn't think it is silly to cry. They can still play together and have lots of fun, but if Jack wants to be sad, she will wait for him until he wants to play again.

FORWARD STEPS

- **TALK**
Tell someone how you are feeling.

- **DO SOMETHING POSITIVE**
Find your own special way to say goodbye.

After Grandma died I told Dad how I wanted to remember her.

I took the day off school and went to the **funeral**. Harry decided to go to school. I cried when they brought Grandma's box into the chapel. It was covered in flowers.

Then we had party food and talked about Grandma. Some cried. Others laughed. Grandma would have loved it with all her family together.

After dark we went outside. Uncle Bob lit the first rocket. It went w-h-o-o-sh up into the sky. And as each rocket went up, Harry and I shouted: 'Bye, Grandma, bye, Grandma.'

I still miss her, but I'm glad I said goodbye in my own special way.

True stories

A NEW SCHOOL

Hello, my name is Maria. My family and I have just moved to a new town. I started a new school today but I don't like it.

I feel really left out. I don't have the right sports kit and I'm not sure what I should have in my pencil case. It is a big school and I keep getting lost. And worst of all, the girl who my teacher paired me up with just wants to play with her own friends. What am I going to do?

I miss my old friends Mark and Katie.

A NEW SCHOOL

Talking it through

It helps to talk to someone...

A PARENT

Maria's mum gives her a hug and says Maria will soon make new friends. She promises to take Maria into town at the weekend to get the right sports kit.

A BIG SISTER

Lauren tells Maria that she has seen some boys and girls her age playing in the park. They are probably from her new school. She offers to take Maria to say hello. Maybe they will let her join in.

A FRIEND

Maria calls Mark. They laugh about his first day at their old school. Mark looked so lonely! Now he has zillions of friends. He says that Maria is good at making friends. She will soon be part of the gang.

FORWARD STEPS

- **JOIN IN**
If you feel lonely ask to join in.

- **SHARE**
Find games that you can play together.

I asked Lauren to take me to the park. I was scared but soon I was playing with two girls from my class.

On Monday I walked to school with Mum. We met my new friends on the way. We chatted so much I think Mum was lonely!

The headteacher welcomed me in assembly and told everyone to remember the Friendship Step in the playground. Children go there if they are looking for someone to play with.

Now my friends and I play hopscotch near the Friendship Step. If there is anyone there, we ask them to join in. My new school helped me feel welcome. Now I welcome other new children.

True stories

MY CLEVER BEST FRIEND

Hi, I'm Sam and my best friend is Dipesh. We're always having fun together. We like going to each other's house to play. Some people think we're twins because we're always doing things together.

When we're at school, I think Dipesh is too brainy. He always wins the prizes. He's the one who gets a smiley face on his work. Teachers like him better than me.

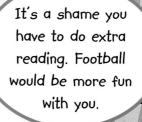

It's a shame you have to do extra reading. Football would be more fun with you.

He knows everything. It's not fair!

Well, we can't all be brainy like you.

I get fed up because I have extra help with my reading. At the same time, Dipesh gets to learn football skills. Then I feel **envious**. I want to be clever like him so I can go outside, too.

If Dipesh wasn't my friend I wouldn't like him. Sometimes I feel really **jealous**. I get cross with him because I have to work extra hard and he doesn't. I don't like being cross. What can I do?

MY CLEVER BEST FRIEND

Talking it through

It helps to talk to someone...

A TEACHER

Mrs Ellis says that everyone has different skills. Sam is good at sports and drawing. She tells Sam that he is great just the way he is and so is Dipesh. That is why they are good friends.

A BIG BROTHER

Jake tells Sam to tell Dipesh how cross he gets and see what Dipesh says. He says that Sam must be clever at some things. He *is* his brother, after all!

A FRIEND

Cheryl says we all have special talents. Sam's is making people laugh in class. He is good at sport, too. She says she likes the way he is always smiling.

FORWARD STEPS

• CHECK IT OUT

Ask how the other person feels.

• THINK

Remember the good things people say about you.

After thinking about it, I told Dipesh I was cross with him for being so clever. I thought Dipesh would be cross back. But he was upset. He said being clever wasn't that great. Some people think he knows everything. Others call him 'boff' and 'geeky'.

He said it doesn't matter if you're clever or thick. What matters is how good a friend you are or how kind you are.

I don't feel **jealous** of Dipesh anymore. I've got talents special to me and Dipesh has talents special to him. Anyway, Dipesh teaches me the football skills he learns.

From now on I'm going to be proud of Dipesh, my special best friend. And I'm going to be proud of myself, too.

Quiz

What would you do?

1. What would you do if, like Charlene, you were jealous of your brother?
a) Act like a little kid.
b) Be cross with him.
c) Talk to your parents.
d) Complain to your friends.

I wish he'd never been born.

2. What would you do if, like Jack, someone you love died?
a) Get cross and blame others.
b) Cry and find a way to remember the person.
c) Forget all about it.
d) Pretend the person is still here.

3. What would you do if, like Maria, you were lonely at your new school?
a) Run away.
b) Hope the problem goes away.
c) Talk your parents into moving back.
d) Make new friends.

4. What would you do if, like Sam, you had a friend who was cleverer than you?

a) Say good things about your friend and you.

b) Say nasty things about your friend.

c) Remember things you hate about your friend.

d) Blame your friend for being too brainy.

He knows everything. It's not fair!

Answers

1.c) Instead of letting jealousy eat away inside you, tell an adult and get them to help you find ways to deal with it.

2.b) Crying helps you to let out the sad feeling you have. When you find your own special way to remember the person it will help you cope better.

3.d) Running away or ignoring the problem will not help. By making new friends you will cope with the sadness of leaving somewhere behind or the fear of moving to a new place.

4.d) Being nasty doesn't stop your friend being clever. But if you say good things about yourself as well as about your friend, you will both be happy.

Glossary

confused

being mixed up, not knowing what to do or think

cover-up feeling

a feeling people use to hide how they are really feeling

emotions

another word for feelings

energy

the power a person needs to get things done

envy or envious

the feeling of wanting to have things other people have

funeral

a few days after a person dies a funeral service is held, often at a church or chapel, to celebrate the person's life

Jamaica

large island country in the Caribbean

jealous or jealousy

the feeling of wanting to be like someone else because the other person is better in some way

loneliness

a feeling of being alone and sorry for yourself

new situations

things that have not happened to a person before – it could be a new school or a first trip in an aeroplane

painful loss

losing something very special to you

real feeling

a real (or authentic) feeling is one of four ways of feeling – this could be; anger, fear, joy or sadness

Find out more

USEFUL BOOKS

Angry Arthur by Hiawyn Oram
When Arthur gets angry he brews up a storm that takes him on a strange journey.

A Volcano In My Tummy by Elaine Whitehouse
A non-fiction book that helps young readers to handle anger.

Badger's Bad Mood by Hiawyn Oram and Badger's Parting Gifts by Susan Varley
Two picture books deal successfully with emotions for younger children.

The English Roses by Madonna
A story for young readers about four girls so jealous of another girl they become unfriendly and mean. Until they find out the facts.

The Huge Bag of Worries by Virginia Ironside
A girl carries her worries around with her. Her gran notices the growing bag and help her to clear it out.

Your Emotions series by Brian Moses
A series of picture books for young children on different feelings.

USEFUL WEBSITES

www.bbc.co.uk/health/kids
Excellent information on what might be worrying children.

www.kidshealth.org
Information for parents and children on feelings and how to deal with them.

www.kidshelp.com.au
A general helpline for children.

USEFUL CONTACTS

Childline
Freepost IIII, London NI 0BR
Helpline: 0800 IIII
www.childline.org.uk

For those children who need to talk to someone outside of their families.

Kidscape
2 Grosvenor Gardens, London, SWIW 0DH
Helpline: 08451 205204
www.kidscape.org.uk
Helps children being bullied or hurt by others.

Index

anger	4, 6-7, 8, 14-15		Jamaica	12, 30
brothers and sisters	8, 11, 12-15, 16		jealousy	5, 8-9, 24–27, 30
cover-up feelings	4-5, 8, 30		joy	4, 8-9
crying	10, 18, 19		loneliness	5, 10-11, 22–23, 30
death	16-19, 30		loss	4, 10, 30
energy	6, 30		love	13, 14
envy	8-9, 25, 30		new school	20-23
excitement	9		new situations	7, 30
fear	4-5, 6-7, 10, 23		real feelings	4-5, 30
'Friendship Step'	23		sadness	4, 10-11, 18
harming people or things	6, 12–15			
hate	12–15			